LEATHER CORDED FUSION TIES

Knotted, Braided & Sinneted Bracelets, Necklaces & Pendants

By JD of *Tying It All Together*

4th Level Indie

ii

**Other Knot Books
By JD of *Tying It All Together***

Decorative Fusion Knots
Paracord Fusion Ties - Volume 1
Paracord Fusion Ties - Volume 2
Paracord Project Inspirations
Paracord Critters

Fusion Ties — Innovative ties created through the merging of different knot elements or knotting techniques.

iii

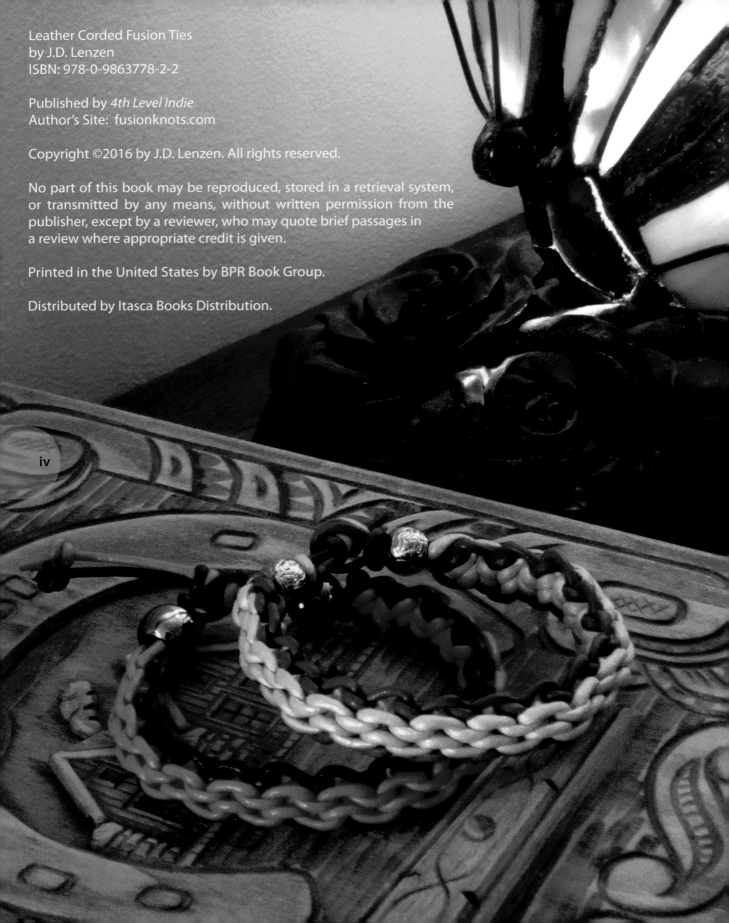

Leather Corded Fusion Ties
by J.D. Lenzen
ISBN: 978-0-9863778-2-2

Published by *4th Level Indie*
Author's Site: fusionknots.com

Printed in the United States by BPR Book Group.

Distributed by Itasca Books Distribution.

Contents

Foreword

I have a deep reverence for knots. My fascination with them and their storied meanings, practical functions and visually poetic possibilities, evolved over different stages of my life. As a child growing up in Seoul, Korea, (traditional) garments and doorways were adorned with Maedeup (Korean knots) and Chinese knots, often symbolizing prosperity or good fortune. They were beautiful, but seemed impossible to tie at the time.

When I joined the U.S. Army, I learned how to tie what would become widely known as the Cobra Stitch. This kept otherwise unwieldy (but incredibly useful) paracord organized and accessible. When we learned to rig equipment for transport and how to tie Swiss Seats with rope for rappelling, I gained an even deeper respect for knots.

Later in life, when I had two children of my own, both with Korean and Irish ancestry, I wished to pass on to them the artistic traditions of their heritage. This was when I first came across books by JD of *Tying It All Together*. I was browsing through a bookstore, looking for historical Celtic and Chinese knots to teach my daughter, when I stumbled upon *Decorative Fusion Knots*. Afterward, I learned about JD's *Paracord Fusion Ties* book series, and picked up volumes I and II. All these books are now staples in our knotting library.

Through JD's books, the complex knots of my childhood were suddenly made simple. Further, my eyes were opened to the fact that beautiful weaves, sinnets and bars were possible beyond the basic Cobra Stitch. Intrigued by the knots and ties JD presented, and inspired to make new knots and ties of my own, I founded *Knotty Origami*—a knotted jewelry business that combines the inspirational insights of JD's books with my core life passions: world culture, form and function, the military and, above all, family.

JD's newest book, *Leather Corded Fusion Ties*, is a staggeringly beautiful compilation of step-by-step (DIY) jewelry designs that merge different knotting and tying techniques using leather cord. You will find uniquely beautiful designs in this book that you won't find elsewhere, like the gorgeous and aptly named Ribcage Braid, one of my personal favorites. However, this is more than just a grouping of DIY leather corded jewelry tutorials. Readers are taught how leather cord is made and provided "need to know" insights for working with leather cord as a design material. This book unravels the mysteries of knots and shows readers how to transform them into impressive, wearable leather jewelry.

JD's clear, well-formatted tutorials have made knot tying accessible to everyone: novice and expert alike. His books and YouTube videos provide the skill backbone for readers and viewers to recreate his designs, and then experiment with and generate new designs of their own. If you have an interest in knots and ties, especially knots and ties that can be used to generate astonishingly beautiful leather corded jewelry, you've selected the right book. Happy tying!

Tricia Driscoll (Knotty Origami, LLC)
Business Owner & Jewelry Designer
knotty-origami.com
October 2015

viii

Introduction

I love leather. I love its smoothness and shine. I love how it feels and how it looks against the skin. I also love knots and ties, or more specifically, designing practical and decorative applications with cord.

This latter love was primarily fostered during the mid 90's, while I was working as a naturalist at an outdoor education school in Loma Mar, California. Outside my teaching responsibilities, I found myself with a lot of time on my hands, and I filled that time with cord. I initially used cord to make knots and ties learned from books. Soon I found myself hungry for more, and so began designing knots and ties of my own. By the late 90's, I'd quietly developed the tying techniques that would come to be known as fusion knotting—the creation of innovative knots and ties through the merging of different knot elements or knotting techniques.

Nearly 20 years later, I've amassed over 400 YouTube instructional knotting videos, written 6 step-by-step instructional knotting books (including the one you are holding now), and have been formally acknowledged by the International Guild of Knot Tyers (IGKT) for my contributions to knotting—an acknowledgment that I will forever treasure.

Always seeking to expand the scope of my corded works and utilize materials that appeal to me and others, I set aside time to design with leather cord.

Leather cord's supple feel, array of available colors and ease of use make it an ideal material for creating a wide variety of knots and ties, especially ones that lend themselves to jewelry pieces. The fruits of those labors are presented here, in *Leather Corded Fusion Ties* (LCFT), a book that shows you how to make wearable, fashionable, high-end leather corded jewelry.

LCFT presents what leather cord has to offer like no other book before. It's focus, the cord itself, demonstrating through detailed step-by-step instructions, how to make 15 elegant and stylish leather corded bracelets, necklaces and pendants, coupled with additional insights showing how to expand those pieces into more (over 25 designs in all).

Still, beyond showing you how to make an expandable number of leather corded jewelry pieces, LCFT endeavors to teach the principles of fusion knotting so that you can start designing and creating new, never before seen, leather corded jewelry pieces of your own.

Because, at its core, this book is not about me and my designs, it is about *you* and *your* inspired creations. The ultimate goal is for you to realize and connect with the creative capabilities present in yourself.

JD of *Tying It All Together*

x

Getting Started

Instruction Format

The intent of this book is to provide all the information necessary to successfully complete each jewelry piece presented while minimizing repetitive procedures. In turn, procedures performed on every knot or tie, such as the use of side cutters or shears, are shown only once (see Equipment Use), and then simply referenced as a procedure to be performed in the instruction text.

In cases where a tying procedure or finishing knot is routinely used, such as the Beaded Wall Knot Start or the Double Overhand Knot, the instruction text calls out the tying procedure or knot to be tied accompanied by the page(s) where that procedure or knot was first shown.

Fusion Ties

Fusion knotting is the creation of innovative knots and ties through the merging of different knot elements or knotting techniques. For example, the Meandering Lark's Head Braid (a fusion tie) is created through the merging of the Lark's Head Knot (knotting technique) and the 4-Strand Round Braid (knotting technique). Together these two component parts create something striking and new (see image below).

The foundation of most fusion ties are built upon historical knotting techniques. In turn, side-by-side with instructions for fusion ties, this book also provides instructions for a handful of bead flourished historical pieces from which knot elements and techniques were utilized to create new unique pieces.

Component Parts

As the term pertains to the book instruction text, component parts are the knot elements or knotting techniques used to make a fusion knot or tie. If an instruction details the creation of a historical knot or tie (see Definitions), the component parts will state "Historical Knot." Otherwise, more information will be provided.

Decoded Subsections

Although this book can be used to generate a fantastic array of leather corded jewelry (over 25 pieces in all), its ultimate goal is to inspire readers to begin creating unique pieces of their own. Guidance for how to do so is presented within each step-by-step instruction. However, as an added bonus, the primary instructions, or elements of those instructions, are further broken down in 8 Decoded subsections dispersed throughout the book. These subsections provide subtle, yet impactful insights leading to additional ties and tie applications.

In short, the Decoded subsections shed light on the nuts and bolts of fusion knotting.

Getting Started

Equipment & Materials

1. Leather Cord: All the leather cords used to create the pieces detailed in this book are round and 2 mm in diameter. Still, smaller (e.g., 1 mm) or larger (e.g., 3 mm) cord diameters work just as well. As with all the recommend equipment and materials, cord can be purchased online, through catalogues, or directly from walk-in (craft, fabric, and/or leather) stores. However, to assure you're using cord of sufficient quality, it is best to purchase directly from an established walk-in store or a reputable, tested and reliable vendor.

The best leather cord is precision cut from the center of a hide. It's smooth, has a soft feel and flexes easily (i.e., it's not too stiff or hard to bend). It should also smell like leather and not chemicals.

On account of a tyer's interest in making a lot of leather corded pieces, it's tempting to purchase large spools or bundles of cord at a time. This is okay, but consider the fact that purchasing bulk amounts of leather cord will increase the chances that a cord has been spliced (i.e., angle cut and glued). Splices are made to increase the length of a spool or bundle of cord, and represent weak points, hidden beneath a layer of leather dye. In turn, purchasing shorter, 8 to 24 ft. (2.4 to 3 m), lengths of cord at a time is recommended and better assures cord quality.

Other cord quality features to note include, the presence of excessive dye (mostly done to cover imperfections) and flaking dye on the surface. The dryness of a cord should also be noted (an indication of a less than ideal cut, poorly treated, or poorly stored cord).

2. Beads: When considering what beads to use for the creation of your pieces, first consider the diameter of the cords being used (e.g., 2 mm). Beads with hole diameters equal to or less than a cord's diameter will be difficult to use. In the case of the designs presented in this book, bead hole sizes of 4 and 5 mm are mostly used (but not always).

Aside from adding an elegant flourish to a knot or tie, beads are also ideal for adding

Getting Started

heft or weight to an otherwise light jewelry piece (e.g., knot pendant necklaces).

3. Small Bowls: Helpful for holding working beads and small scraps of cord.

4. Scratch Awl: Technically, a scratch awl is used for marking a piece of leather or wood. Nevertheless, this same tool is also usefully for widening the space through the center of a bead, laced with 2 mm leather cords. This latter (book specific) use of a scratch awl is illustrated on Page xv.

5. Super Fine Chain Nose Pliers: These are traditionally used when working with wire, closing jump rings and bead tips or attaching various findings. But, these same pliers are also great for working with leather cord. For the purposes of this book, they help to pull cord ends through tightly packed beads. This use is illustrated on Page xv.

6. Barber Shears: A well sharpened pair of barber shears will be all you need to cover most of your trimming and/or

cutting needs (see Page xvi). In all other cases the super fine side cutters described below should do the trick.

7. Super Fine Side Cutters: These are cutters with a sharp-angled jaw used to create a clean cut in tight places. The need for clean, close, cord cuts at the top of a bead, prior to tying a locking transition knot (e.g., 2-Strand Wall Knot), make super fine side cutters a "must have" piece of equipment to own. Their use is illustrated on Page xvi.

8. Measuring Tape or Ruler: Needed to measure lengths or sections of leather cord prior to and during a project tie, and to approximate loop and bead hole diameters.

xiv

Equipment Use

Use of Scratch Awl

1. When the cords laced through the center of a bead impede the insertion of an additional cord…

2. …carefully press the scratch awl through the bead, between or above the laced cords.

3. In most cases, this action will open up enough space to enable you to press the additional cord…

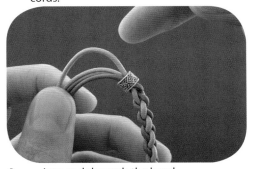

4. …into and through the bead.

Use of Super Fine Chain Nose Pliers

1. In cases when a cord enters a bead, but only exits the bead's other end slightly or becomes stuck…

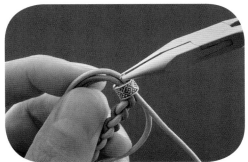

2. …use the chain nose pliers to grip the short cord end. Then pull the rest of the cord length through the bead.

Equipment Use (continued)

Use of Super Fine Side Cutters

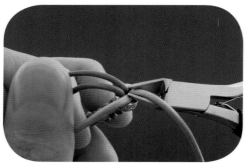

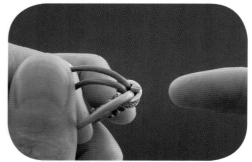

1. If a clean, close, cord cut is needed atop a bead, side cutters should be used.

2. However, take care to only cut the cord of interest, and not nip or cut other cords with the side cutter tips.

Use of Barber Shears

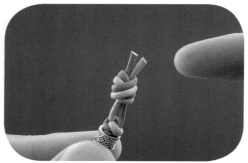

1. In most cases (aside from the case illustrated above), a well sharpened pair of barber shears…

2. …will be all you need to complete cord cuts.

Useful Clarifications
<u>Visual Information</u>

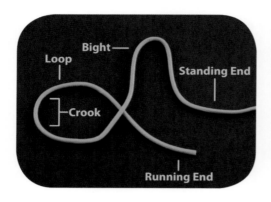 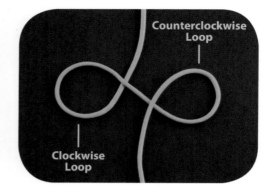

<u>Definitions</u>

ABOK: Acronym for *The Ashley Book of Knots*.

Bar: A semi-rigid, tightly constructed tie typically (but not always) made with square knots (e.g., Aztec Sun Bar).

Bight: A line doubled over into a U-shape.

Circle: A line making one complete revolution around another line or body part (e.g., finger).

Clockwise Loop: A loop that has a running end (or line on top) that rotates clockwise.

Coil: A line that makes several (more than one) revolutions around another line or body part (e.g., finger).

Component Part: A knot element or knotting technique used to make a fusion knot or tie.

Concentric: Denoting circles, arcs, or other shapes that share the same center.

Cord: A slender length of flexible material used to make a knot or tie.

Counterclockwise Loop: A loop that has a running end (or line on top) that rotates counterclockwise.

CRB: Acronym for the term Customizable Round Braid.

Crook: The curved inside part of a bight, circle, loop, or hooked line.

Doubled: Two lines worked with in parallel to one another, immediately side-by-side.

Firm: The point at which the adjusting of a knot results in a satisfactory appearance.

Flip: Turning a knot, tie, or semi-completed knot or tie over, upside down, vertically, or horizontally.

Fusion Tie: An innovative tie created through the merging of different knot elements or knotting techniques.

xviii

Getting Started

Historical Knot: Knots that were discovered or created before 1979 (the year the IGKT updated ABOK).

Hook: A line that makes a sharp curve or a shape resembling a hook, typically around a line.

IGKT: Acronym for the International Guild of Knot Tyers.

Lace: A threaded cord used to tie together opposite ends.

LCFT: Acronym for the book *Leather Corded Fusion Ties*.

Legs: Dangling or vertical parallel cords.

Line: The material used to tie a knot or tie (e.g., leather cord, rope, wire, etc.).

Lock: To fasten or secure something in place.

Loop: A circle of line that crosses itself, or a bight cinched at its base.

P: A line that is looped to look like the letter P or the mirror image of the letter P.

Parallel: Two straight lines or cords maintaining an equal distance from one another.

Piece: The partially completed or final version of an entire knot or tie.

Rounded: A knot or tie molded to have a curved surface or spherical shape.

Running End: The end of a line that's being used to make the knot or tie.

Sinnet: A weaving technique or tie generally (but not always) performed with a series of slip knots, used to shorten the length of a line.

Splay: To spread two or more lines outward or away from one another.

Stabilized: A knot or tie that has had its shape or structure fixed or secured by another knotting technique.

Standing End: The end of a line that is not involved in making the knot or tie.

Start: A knotting technique or procedure performed at the beginning of a tie (e.g., Beaded Wall Knot Start).

TIAT: Acronym for the YouTube video channel *Tying It All Together*.

Tuck: Inserting a line or bight through a loop or under another line.

U: A line that is shaped to look like the letter U.

Beaded Snake Knot

Cords Used: One 7 ft. (2.1 m), 2 mm Dia. Cord

Piece Size: 7.5 in. (19.1 cm) Bracelet

Beads Used: Eight 8x5 mm Cylindrical Beads, 5 mm Dia. Hole (Geometric Pattern)

Component Parts: Historical Knot + Bead Flourishes

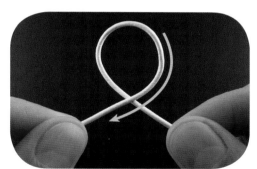

1. At the middle of the cord, make a **2-Strand Wall Knot**: Cross the right cord end over the left.

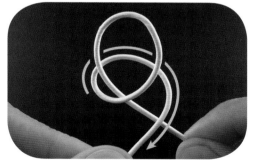

2. Then hook the left running end right, around the back of, and over, the other cord end.

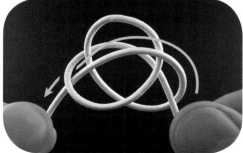

3. Now hook the right running end left, through the front of the left crook.

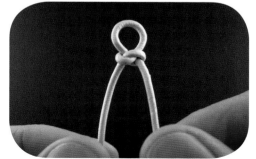

4. Adjust the cords until the Wall Knot is firm. Leave a 0.375 in. (0.95 cm) loop on top when tying the start (only).

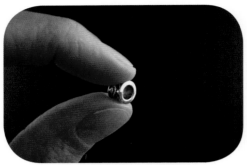

5. Grab a bead with a 5 mm hole (minimum hole size)…

6. …and place it around both cord ends, beneath the Wall Knot. **Note:** Beaded Wall Knot Start shown.

7. Repeat Steps 1 through 4 five times, generating a Snake Knot (i.e., a series of stacked Wall Knots).

8. Place a bead (see Step 5) around both cord ends, beneath the Snake Knot.

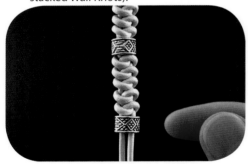

9. Repeat Steps 7 and 8 until a minimum 10 in. (25.4 cm) of cord ends remain.

10. Then firmly tie a 2-Strand Wall Knot (see Page 1) beneath, and snugly against, the last placed bead.

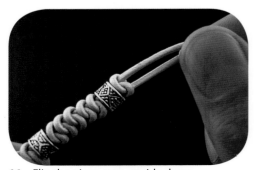

11. Flip the piece over, upside down.

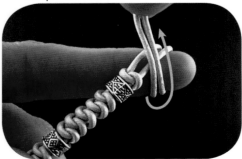

12. **Double Overhand Knot:** Circle the cord ends around the standing ends and your index finger…

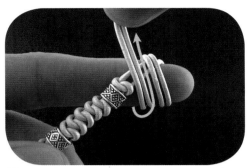

13. …twice, making sure the loops created remain parallel to one another.

14. Drop the cord ends down, behind your index finger…

15. Then insert them up and through the parallel loops created.

16. Adjust the cords until the Double Overhand Knot is firm and located 0.25 in. (0.64 cm) above the Wall Knot.

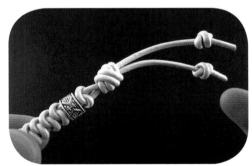

17. To create a dangling knot finish to the ball and loop clasp, repeat Steps 12 through 16 along each (single) cord end.

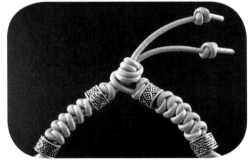

18. Or, see the Decoded subsection on Page 15 for an alternate tying method.

19. To create a traditional finish to the ball and loop clasp…

20. …carefully snip both cord ends 0.25 in. (0.64 cm) above the Double Overhand Knot.

Divided Double Coin Knot

Cords Used:	Two 4 ft. (1.2 m), 2 mm Dia. Cord
Piece Size:	7.5 in. (19.1 cm) Bracelet
Beads Used:	Two 10x8 mm Rounded Beads, 5 mm Dia. Hole (Harmonic Wave Pattern); Two 8x9 mm Cylindrical Beads, 5 mm Dia. Hole (Compressed Wave Pattern)
Component Parts:	4-Strand Flat Braid + Double Coin Knot + Contrasting Cords + Bead Flourishes

4

1. At the middle of the first cord, tie the Beaded Wall Knot Start (see Pages 1 and 2).

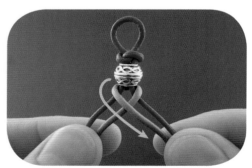

2. At the middle of the second cord, firmly cross the left cord end over the right, in front of and between the legs of the other cord.

3. Firmly cross the upper cords, left over right, in front of and between the legs below.

4. Again, firmly cross the upper cords, left over right, in front of and between the legs below.

5. Repeat Steps 3 and 4 until approximately 1 in. (2.5 cm) short of the middle of the piece [example tied to 2.5 in. (6.4 cm)].

6. Place a bead with a 5 mm hole (minimum hole size) around all four cords.

7. Make sure the middlemost cords in Step 5 are on top of the upper cords in Step 5.

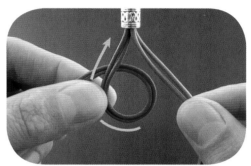

8. **Double Coin Knot:** Make a clockwise **P** with the left doubled cord ends.

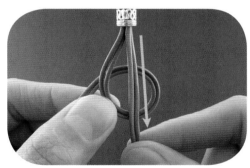

9. Drop the right doubled cord ends down over the loop of the **P**.

10. Hook the right (doubled) running ends left, under the leg of the **P**.

11. Then bight the running ends and weave them over, under, over, and under the doubled cords to the right.

12. Pull the bight out to form the (Divided) Double Coin Knot.

5

13. Adjust the cord ends until the Double Coin Knot is firm.

14. Cross the doubled cord ends, left over right.

15. Place a bead (see Step 6) around all four cord ends.

16. Then splay the cord ends out, making sure the right cords in Step 14 are on top of the left cords in Step 14.

17. Firmly cross the upper cords, right over left, behind and between the legs below.

18. Again, firmly cross the upper cords, right over left, behind and between the legs below.

19. Repeat Steps 17 and 18 until a minimum 10 in. (25.4 cm) of cord ends remain.

20. Place a bead (see Step 6) around all four cords.

21. Make sure the middlemost cords in Step 19 are on top of the upper cords in Step 19.

22. Flip the piece over, upside down and splay the cord ends out as shown.

23. Carefully snip the lower left and upper right cord ends at the bead.

24. Firmly tie a 2-Strand Wall Knot (see Page 1) snugly atop the bead, with the remaining cords.

25. Tie a Double Overhand Knot (see Pages 2 and 3) 0.25 in. (0.64 cm) above the Wall Knot.

26. Carefully snip both cord ends 0.25 in. (0.64 cm) above the Double Overhand Knot.

Customizable Round Braid

Cords Used: Two 8 ft. (2.4 m), 2 mm Dia. Cord

Piece Size: 1 in. (2.5 cm) Dia. Single Loop Design; 2.5 ft. (0.8 m) Necklace

Beads Used: Two 8x10 mm Barrel Beads, 5 mm Dia. Hole (Flower Pattern); One 11x14 mm Cylindrical Bead, 8 mm Dia. Hole (Spiraled S Pattern) *

Bead seen in image of completed piece.

Component Parts: 4-Strand Round Braid + Transitioning Technique + Various Loop Configurations

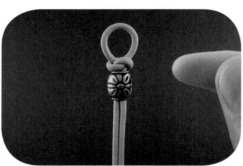

1. At the middle of the first cord, tie the Beaded Wall Knot Start (see Pages 1 and 2).

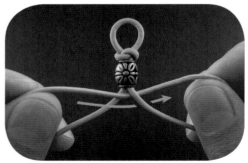

2. Lace the middle of the second cord over the left leg and under the right leg of the other cord.

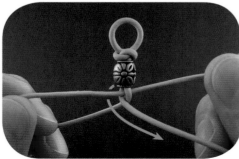

3. Firmly cross the lower left cord over the lower right cord, under the outstretched cord above.

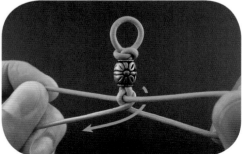

4. Firmly cross the upper right cord over the upper left cord, under the crossed cords below.

5. Firmly cross the upper left cord over the upper right cord, under the crossed cords below.

6. Repeat Steps 4 and 5 until…

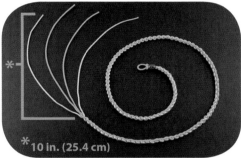

*10 in. (25.4 cm)

7. …a minimum 10 in. (25.4 cm) of cord ends remain (cord lengths required to complete finishing knot).

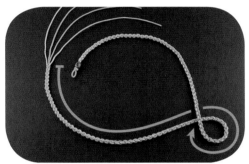

8. Loop the braid at each transition point (determined by the number, size, and location of the loops in your design).

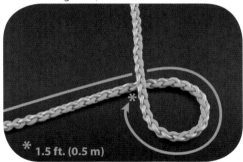

* 1.5 ft. (0.5 m)

9. Measure the distances back to each transition point. **Note:** The example shown is for a one loop design.

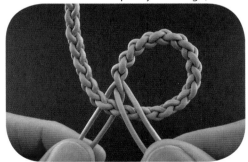

10. Untie the braid back to the first transition point. **Transitioning Tech.:** Splay the cord ends over the braid in the Step 5 orientation.

11. Firmly cross the upper right cord over the upper left cord, under the braid.

12. Firmly cross the upper left cord over the upper right cord, under the crossed cords below.

13. Firmly cross the upper right cord over the upper left cord, under the crossed cords below.

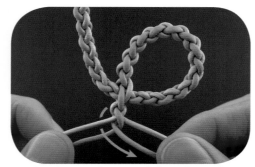

14. Firmly cross the upper left cord over the upper right cord, under the crossed cords below.

15. Repeat Steps 13 and 14 until the next transition point (see Step 10) or a minimum 10 in. (25.4 cm) of cord ends remain.

16. Hook the upper left cord right, between the crossed cords below.

17. Place a bead with a 5 mm hole (minimum hole size) around all four cords, maintaining their adjusted positions.

18. Flip the piece over, upside down and splay the cord ends out as shown.

19. Carefully snip the lower left and upper right cord ends at the bead.

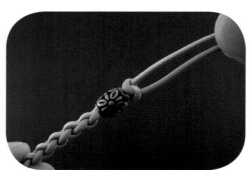

20. Firmly tie a 2-Strand Wall Knot (see Page 1) snugly atop the bead, with the remaining cords.

21. Tie a Double Overhand Knot (see Pages 2 and 3) 0.25 in. (0.64 cm) above the Wall Knot.

22. Carefully snip both cord ends 0.25 in. (0.64 cm) above the Double Overhand Knot.

DECODED
Customizable Round Braid Options

Generally speaking, a knotting design is "customizable" when its component parts can be adjusted into a variety of configurations according to the tyer's interests. In the case of the Customizable Round Braid (CRB), a variety of loop configurations can be generated by changing the number of times a transitioning technique is used, coupled with the location, size, and complexity of the loops created. Below are a handful of CRB loop configurations you might like to try.

1. Single loop design, as shown in the preceding step-by-step [loop size = 1 in. (2.5 cm)].

2. Double loop design, two concentric loops [loop sizes: large = 1 in. (2.5 cm); small = 0.5 in. (1.3 cm)].

3. Double loop design, nautilus shape, outer loop pulled [loop sizes: large = (initially) 1 in. (2.5 cm); small = 0.5 in. (1.3 cm)].

4. Triple loop design, large loop centered below two small loops [loop sizes: large =1 in. (2.5 cm); small = 0.5 in. (1.3 cm)].

11

Beaded Snake Weave

Cords Used: Two 4 ft. (1.2 m), 2 mm Dia. Cord

Piece Size: 7.5 in. (19.1 cm) Bracelet

Beads Used: Two 10x8 mm Rounded Beads, 5 mm Dia. Hole (Rose Pattern); Four 7x12 mm Barrel Beads, 4 mm Dia. Hole (S & Dot Pattern)

Component Parts: Historical Knot + Contrasting Cords + Bead Flourishes

12

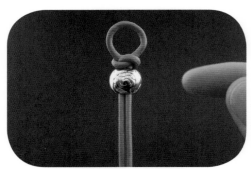

1. At the middle of the first cord, tie the Beaded Wall Knot Start (see Pages 1 and 2).

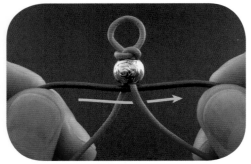

2. Lace the middle of the second cord over the left leg and under the right leg of the other cord.

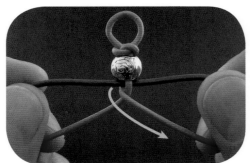

3. Firmly cross the lower left cord over the lower right cord, under the outstretched cord above.

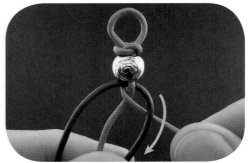

4. Cross the upper right cord left, over the lower right cord.

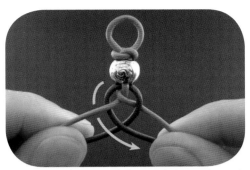

5. Weave the upper left cord right, under and over the cords beneath it.

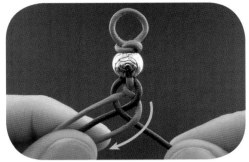

6. Cross the upper right cord left, over the lower right cord.

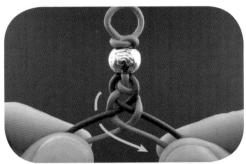

7. Weave the upper left cord right, under and over the cords beneath it.

8. Repeat Steps 4 through 7 one more time.

9. Place a bead with a 4 mm hole (minimum hole size) around the middlemost cords.

10. Cross the upper right cord (above the bead) left, over the lower right cord (below the bead).

11. Weave the upper left cord (above the bead) right, under and over the cords beneath it.

12. Repeat Steps 6 and 7.

13. Repeat Steps 4 through 7 one more time.

14. Repeat Steps 9 through 13 until a minimum 10 in. (25.4 cm) of cord ends remain.

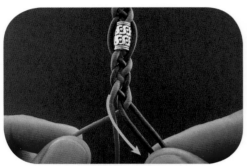

15. Cross the upper left cord right, over the middlemost cords, aligning it beneath and beside the upper right cord.

16. Make sure the leftmost cords remain crossed.

17. Place a bead with a 5 mm hole (minimum hole size) around all four cords, maintaining their adjusted positions.

18. Flip the piece over, upside down and splay the cord ends out as shown.

19. Carefully snip the lower left and upper right cord ends at the bead.

20. Firmly tie a 2-Strand Wall Knot (see Page 1) snugly atop the bead, with the remaining cords.

21. Tie a Double Overhand Knot (see Pages 2 and 3) 0.25 in. (0.64 cm) above the Wall Knot.

22. Carefully snip both cord ends 0.25 in. (0.64 cm) above the Double Overhand Knot.

DECODED
Double Overhand Knot - Single Cord

The technique presented on Pages 2 and 3, showing how to tie a Double Overhand Knot with two cords (around your finger), is sufficient for creating a Double Overhand Knot on a single cord. But sometimes, having enough cord to wrap around your finger is in short supply, especially at the end of a piece. So here's an alternative tying method that requires less cord to generate the same knot (on a single cord).

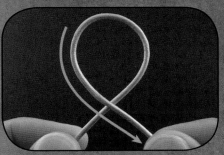

1. Make a counterclockwise loop in the cord.

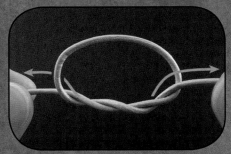

2. Insert the left cord end through the front of the left crook and the right cord end through the back of the right crook.

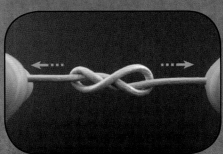

3. Then pull both cord ends, at the same time, until the loop collapses on itself, generating the shape of a figure eight.

4. Keep pulling on the cord ends until the Double Overhand Knot is rounded and firm.

Bead Bound Double Coin Knot

Cords Used: One 4 ft. (1.2 m), 2 mm Dia. Cord

Piece Size: 1 in. (2.5 cm) Dia. Pendant; 2.5 ft. (0.8 m) Adjustable Length Necklace

Beads Used: Four 7x9 mm Cylindrical Beads, 4 mm Dia. Hole (Reflected S Pattern)

Component Parts: Historical Knot + Bead Stabilization + Bead Flourishes

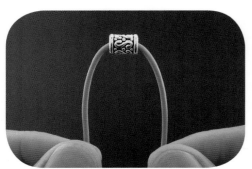

1. Bight the middle of the cord and place a bead with a 4 mm hole (minimum hole size) around its top.

2. Make a clockwise **P** with the left cord end and place a bead (see Step 1) around its loop.

3. Drop the right cord end down over the loop of the **P**, left of the bead.

4. Hook the right running end left, under the leg of the **P**.

5. Place a bead (see Step 1) around it, above the leg of the **P**.

6. Then bight the running end and weave it over, under, over, and under the cords (and beads) to the right.

7. Pull the bight out to form the Double Coin Knot.

8. Adjust the cord ends until the beads are evenly spaced and the Double Coin Knot is firm.

9. **Ladder Stitching:** Place a bead (see Step 1) around the base of the right cord end.

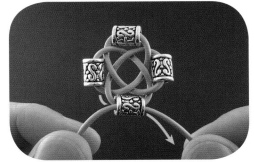

10. Insert the left cord end through the (horizontally orientated) bead, under the other cord end.

11. Flip the piece over, upside down, and make any final adjustments (if needed).

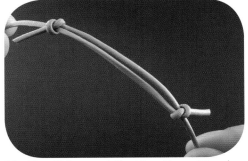

12. Tie a Fisherman's Knot (see Pages 23 and 24) with the cord ends to generate an adjustable necklace.

Ribcage Braid

Cords Used: One 6 ft. (1.8 m) & One 4 ft. (1.2 m), 2 mm Dia. Cord

Piece Size: 7.5 in. (19.1 cm) Bracelet

Beads Used: Two 8x9 mm Cylindrical Beads, 5 mm Dia. Hole (Compressed Wave Pattern)

Component Parts: Opposing Single Cord Loops + Snake Weave + Contrasting Cords + Bead Flourishes

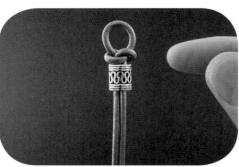

1. At the middle of the first cord, tie the Beaded Wall Knot Start (see Pages 1 and 2).

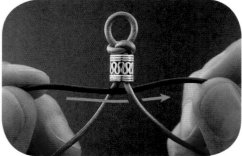

2. Lace the middle of the short cord over the left leg and under the right leg of the other cord.

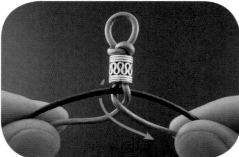

3. Firmly cross the lower left cord over the lower right cord, under the outstretched cord above.

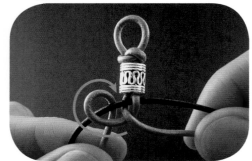

4. Circle the middlemost left cord over and around the front of the outer left cord.

5. Circle the middlemost right cord under and around the back of the outer right cord.

6. Firmly cross the middlemost cords, left over right.

7. Repeat Steps 4 through 6 one more time.

8. Cross the outer right cord left, over the middlemost right cord.

9. Weave the outer left cord right, under and over the cords beneath it.

10. Cross the upper right cord left, over the lower right cord.

11. Weave the upper left cord right, under and over the cords beneath it.

12. Repeat Steps 4 through 11 until a minimum 10 in. (25.4 cm) of cord ends remain.

13. Cross the upper left cord right, over the middlemost cords, aligning it beneath and beside the upper right cord.

14. Make sure the leftmost cords remain crossed.

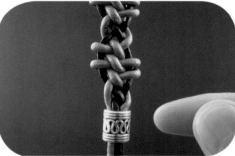

15. Place a bead with a 5 mm hole (minimum hole size) around all four cords, maintaining their adjusted positions.

16. Flip the piece over, upside down and splay the cord ends out as shown.

17. Carefully snip the lower left and upper right cord ends at the bead.

18. Firmly tie a 2-Strand Wall Knot (see Page 1) snugly atop the bead, with the remaining cords.

19. Tie a Double Overhand Knot (see Pages 2 and 3) 0.25 in. (0.64 cm) above the Wall Knot.

20. Carefully snip both cord ends 0.25 in. (0.64 cm) above the Double Overhand Knot.

20

Celtic Heart Knot

Cords Used: One 4 ft. (1.2 m) & One 2 ft. (0.6 m), 2 mm Dia. Cord

Piece Size: 1 in. (2.5 cm) Dia. Pendant; 2.5 ft. (0.8 m) Adjustable Length Necklace

Beads Used: One 10x8 mm Rounded Bead, 5 mm Dia. Hole (Harmonic Wave Pattern)

Component Parts: Historical Knot + Bead Flourish

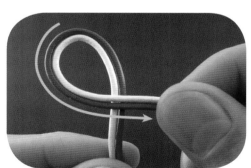

1. At the middle of both cords, doubled (short cord on top of long), make a counterclockwise loop.

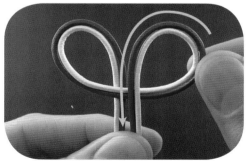

2. Make a second counterclockwise loop to the right of the first.

3. Tuck the right loop under and through the left loop.

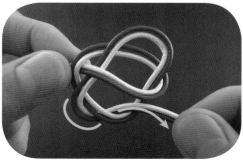

4. Hook the running ends (i.e., dangling doubled cords) up, under, and through the crook above it.

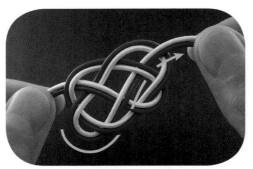

5. Then weave the running ends diagonally right, over, under, and over the doubled cords above it.

6. Adjust the cord ends until the Celtic Heart Knot is firm.

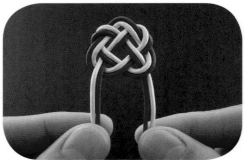

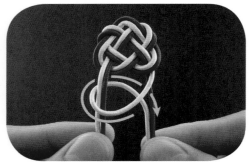

7. Flip the piece over, upside down.

8. **2-Strand Wall Knot - Around Cords:** Make a counterclockwise loop, with the outer right cord, around the left doubled cord ends.

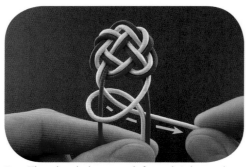

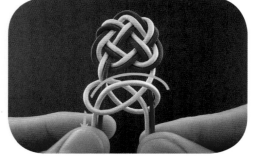

9. Then hook the outer left cord right, under the right doubled cord ends.

10. Now hook the same cord left, through the front of the left crook.

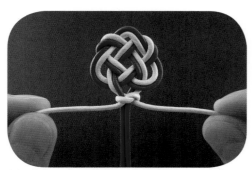

11. Adjust the cords until the Wall Knot is firm.

12. Drop the running ends of the Wall Knot down, outside the middlemost cords.

13. Place a bead with a 5 mm hole (minimum hole size) around all four cords.

14. Flip the piece over, upside down and splay the cord ends out as shown.

15. Carefully snip the lower left and upper right cord ends at the bead.

16. Firmly tie a 2-Strand Wall Knot (see Page 1) snugly atop the bead, with the remaining cords.

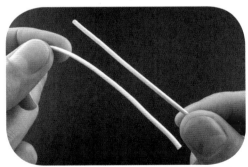

17. **Fisherman's Knot:** Line up the cord ends, side-by-side.

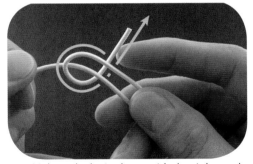

18. Make a clockwise loop, with the right cord end, around the left cord end.

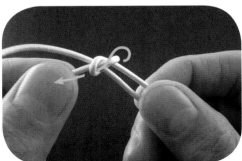

19. Then insert the right cord end through the loop.

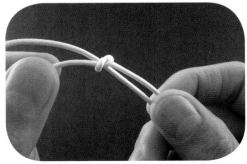

20. Tighten the Overhand Knot made firmly.

23

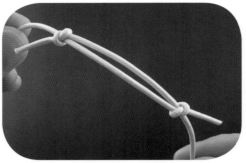

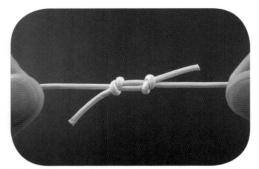

21. Flip the piece over, upside down, and repeat Steps 18 through 20.

22. Pull on the long ends to expand, and the short ends to reduce, the length of the necklace cord.

DECODED
Streamlined Ties

All the book ties that integrate strategically placed beads or a (loop incorporating) transition technique can also be tied without such flourishes. The resulting appearance of these ties will be more streamlined, such that the completed bracelet, choker or necklace will take on a simpler, more traditional look. For inspiration, the following images show what two book ties would look like without the incorporation of bead flourishes.

1. **Aztec Sun Bar:** Follow the steps presented on Pages 39 through 42, with the exception of Step 9 and all references to Step 9.

2. **Snake Weave:** Follow the steps presented on Pages 12 through 15, with the exception of Step 9 and all references to Step 9.

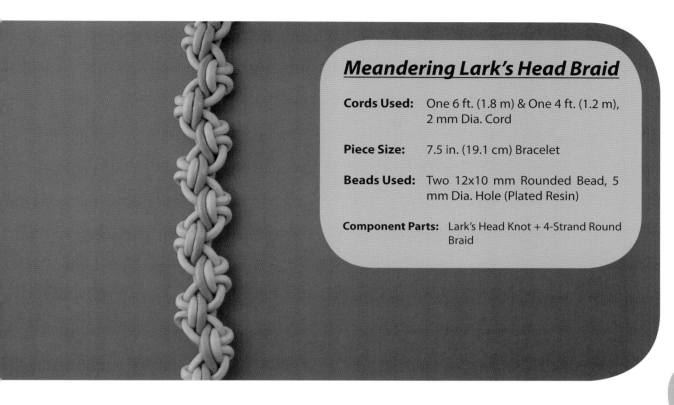

Meandering Lark's Head Braid

Cords Used: One 6 ft. (1.8 m) & One 4 ft. (1.2 m), 2 mm Dia. Cord

Piece Size: 7.5 in. (19.1 cm) Bracelet

Beads Used: Two 12x10 mm Rounded Bead, 5 mm Dia. Hole (Plated Resin)

Component Parts: Lark's Head Knot + 4-Strand Round Braid

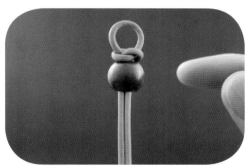

1. At the middle of the first cord, tie the Beaded Wall Knot Start (see Pages 1 and 2).

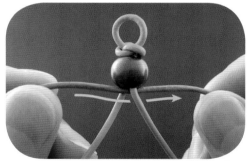

2. Lace the middle of the short cord over the left leg and under the right leg of the other cord.

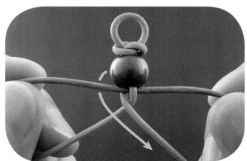

3. Firmly cross the lower left cord over the lower right cord, under the outstretched cord above.

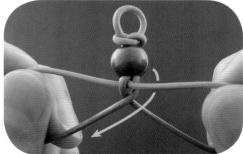

4. Firmly cross the upper right cord over the upper left cord, under the crossed cords below.

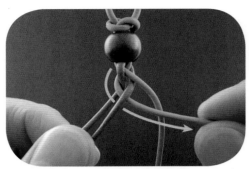

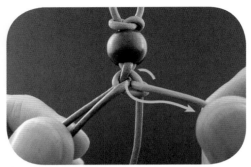

5. Hook the outer left cord right, between the crossed cords below, and over the outer right cord.

6. Then circle it around the back of the outer right cord, exiting above itself.

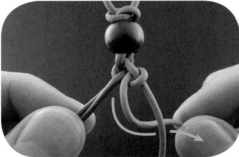

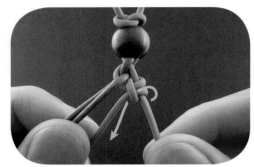

7. Hook the same cord under the outer right cord. Then circle it…

8. …around the front of the outer right cord, and through the crook below. Firmly tighten the Lark's Head made.

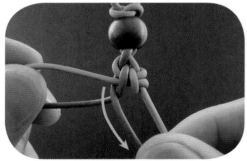

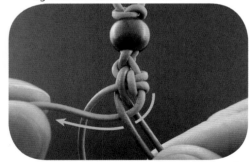

9. Firmly cross the back left cord over the front left cord, under the cord below.

10. Hook the outer right cord left, between the crossed cords below, and over the outer left cord.

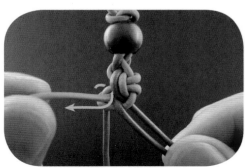

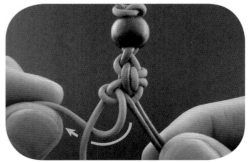

11. Then circle it around the back of the outer left cord, exiting above itself.

12. Hook the same cord under the outer left cord. Then circle it…

26

13. …around the front of the outer left cord, and through the crook below. Firmly tighten the Lark's Head made.

14. Firmly cross the back right cord over the front right cord, under the cord below.

15. Repeat Steps 5 through 14 until a minimum 10 in. (25.4 cm) of cord ends remain.

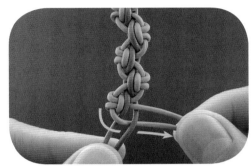

16. Hook the outer left cord right, between the crossed cords below.

17. Place a bead with a 5 mm hole (minimum hole size) around all four cords, maintaining their adjusted positions.

18. Flip the piece over, upside down and splay the cord ends out as shown.

19. Carefully snip the lower left and upper right cord ends at the bead.

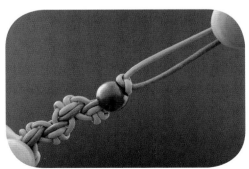

20. Firmly tie a 2-Strand Wall Knot (see Page 1) snugly atop the bead, with the remaining cords.

21. Tie a Double Overhand Knot (see Pages 2 and 3) 0.25 in. (0.64 cm) above the Wall Knot.

22. Carefully snip both cord ends 0.25 in. (0.64 cm) above the Double Overhand Knot.

DECODED

Bead Bound Knots

As seen in the instructions for the Bead Bound Double Coin Knot, bead binding is a great way to stabilize the frame of a flat knot. The strategically placed beads hold the knot's shape and horizontal position, keeping it parallel to the cords above. Because of this, bead binding a knot can help make it more ideal as a necklace pendant, or, as the information below illustrates, a fantastic looking bracelet, choker, or necklace (depending on the length of cord and the number of beads used).

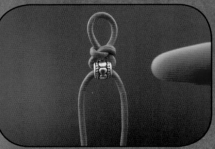

1. At the middle of the cord tie a Beaded Wall Knot Start (see Pages 1 and 2), Ladder Stitching (see Page 17) the bead.

2. Follow Steps 2 through 10 on Pages 16 and 17.

3. Repeat Steps 2 through 10 on Pages 16 and 17 until a minimum 10 in. (25.4 cm) of cord ends remain.

4. Tie a Double Overhand Knot (see Pages 2 and 3) 0.25 in. (0.64 cm) below the last placed bead.

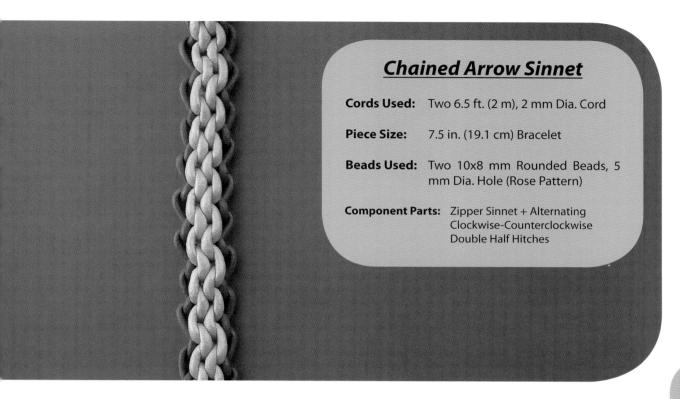

Chained Arrow Sinnet

Cords Used: Two 6.5 ft. (2 m), 2 mm Dia. Cord

Piece Size: 7.5 in. (19.1 cm) Bracelet

Beads Used: Two 10x8 mm Rounded Beads, 5 mm Dia. Hole (Rose Pattern)

Component Parts: Zipper Sinnet + Alternating Clockwise-Counterclockwise Double Half Hitches

1. At the middle of the first cord, tie the Beaded Wall Knot Start (see Pages 1 and 2).

2. Flip the piece over, upside down.

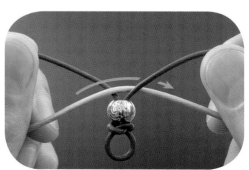

3. Lace the middle of the second cord over the left leg and under the right leg of the other cord.

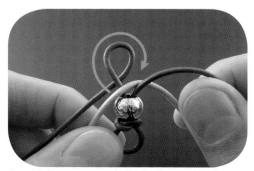

4. Make a counterclockwise loop with the outer left cord.

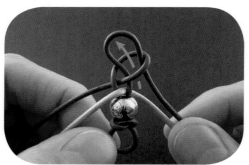

5. Bight the outer right cord through the left loop…

6. …and tighten, leaving a 0.5 in. (1.3 cm) loop in the Slip Knot made.

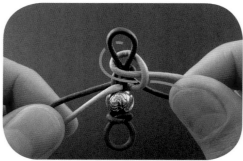

7. Make a clockwise loop with the middlemost right cord, around the loop above.

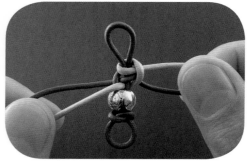

8. Tighten the clockwise loop firmly.

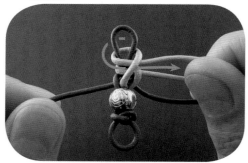

9. Make a clockwise loop with the middlemost left cord, around the loop above.

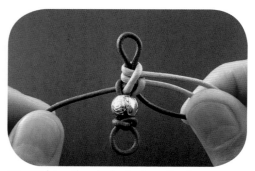

10. Tighten the clockwise loop firmly.

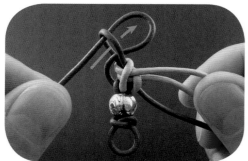

11. Bight the outer left cord through the right loop…

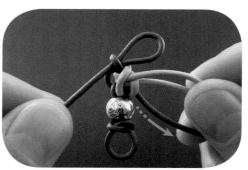

12. …and tighten, leaving a 0.5 in. (1.3 cm) loop in the Slip Knot made.

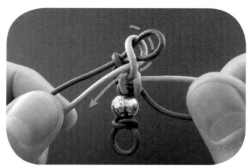

13. Make a counterclockwise loop with the middlemost left cord, around the loop above.

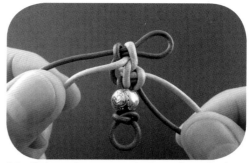

14. Tighten the counterclockwise loop firmly.

15. Make a counterclockwise loop with the middlemost right cord, around the loop above.

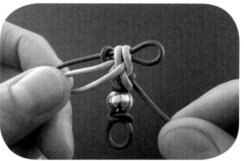

16. Tighten the counterclockwise loop firmly.

17. Repeat Steps 5 through 16 until a minimum 10 in. (25.4 cm) of cord ends remain.

18. Then insert the middlemost cords and the outer right cord through the loop above…

19. …and tighten firmly.

20. Flip the piece over, upside down. Then place a bead with a 5 mm hole (minimum hole size) around all four cords.

21. Make sure the middlemost cords in Step 19 are on top of the outer cords in Step 19.

22. Flip the piece over, upside down and splay the cord ends out as shown.

23. Carefully snip the lower left and upper right cord ends at the bead.

24. Firmly tie a 2-Strand Wall Knot (see Page 1) snugly atop the bead, with the remaining cords.

25. Tie a Double Overhand Knot (see Pages 2 and 3) 0.25 in. (0.64 cm) above the Wall Knot.

26. Carefully snip both cord ends 0.25 in. (0.64 cm) above the Double Overhand Knot.

Royal Butterfly Knot

Cords Used: One 4 ft. (1.2 m), 2 mm Dia. Cord

Piece Size: 1.5 in. (3.8 cm) Wide Pendant; 2.5 ft. (0.8 m) Adjustable Length Necklace

Beads Used: One 12x13 mm Cylindrical Bead, 5 mm Dia. Hole (Linked Loop Pattern)

Component Parts: Trinity Knot + Opposing Half Hitches + Bead Flourish

1. Bight the middle of the cord and place a bead with a 5 mm hole (minimum hole size) around its top.

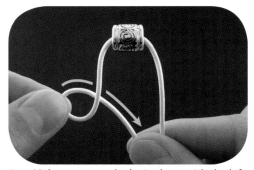

2. Make a counterclockwise loop with the left cord end.

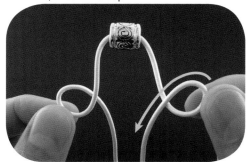

3. Make a counterclockwise loop with the right cord end.

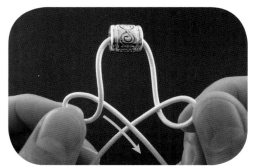

4. Cross the left cord end over the right.

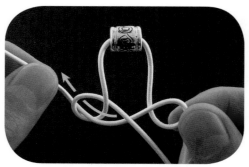

5. Insert the cord on the left through the front of the left loop.

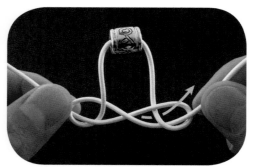

6. Insert the cord on the right through the back of the right loop.

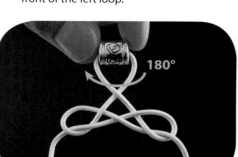

7. Rotate the bead 180° to the left, horizontally, making a counterclockwise loop below.

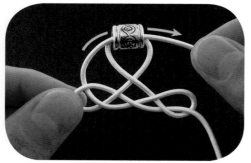

8. Insert the left cord through the bead, atop the loop below.

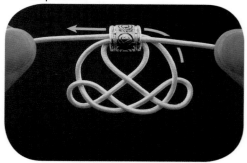

9. Insert the right cord through the bead, under the left cord.

10. Expand the loops to the left and right of the top loop, until they are slightly wider than the loops below.

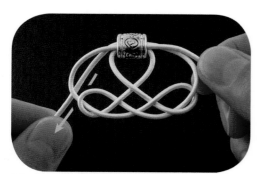

11. Drop the left cord end down under the large left loop.

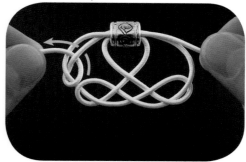

12. Then circle it around the front of the outer left cord, under itself, and over the edge of the outer left cord.

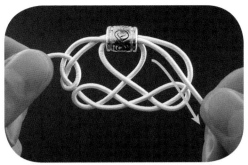

13. Drop the right cord end down over the large right loop.

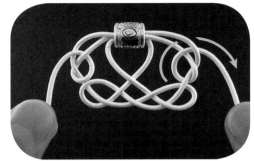

14. Then circle it around the back of the outer right cord, over itself, and under the edge of the outer right cord.

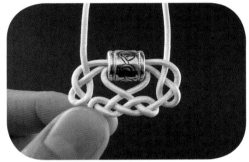

15. Adjust the cord ends until the Royal Butterfly Knot is firm.

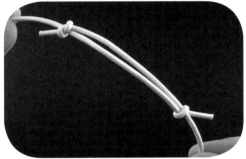

16. Tie a Fisherman's Knot (see Pages 23 and 24) with the cord ends to generate an adjustable necklace.

DECODED
Bracelets as Chokers & Necklaces

Every bracelet shown in this book can be converted into a choker or necklace. All that needs to be done is increase the length of cord used to generate the original bracelet (in consideration of the wearer's neck size and/or the desired length of the final piece). The following are ideas for a choker and necklace, including their respective additional cord lengths used.

1. Ribcage Braid Choker: Follow the steps presented on Pages 18 through 20, increasing each cord length used ~ 3 times.

2. Snake Knot Necklace: Follow the steps presented on Pages 1 through 3, increasing the cord length used ~ 4 times.

Beaded Ashoka Chakra Knot

Cords Used: One 6 ft. (1.8 m), 2 mm Dia. Cord

Piece Size: 2 in. (5 cm) Dia. Pendant; 2.5 ft. (0.8 m) Adjustable Length Necklace

Beads Used: Thirteen 7x6 mm Barrel Beads, 4 mm Dia. Hole (Dot Pattern); Two 7x12 mm Barrel, 4 mm Dia. Hole (S & Dot Pattern)

Component Parts: Slip Knot Loop + Repeating Slip Knots + Bead Flourishes

36

1. Approximately 1 ft. (0.3 m) right of the middle of the cord, make a counterclockwise loop.

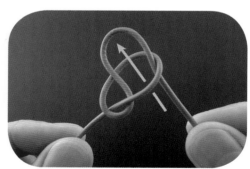

2. Bight the right running end through the loop…

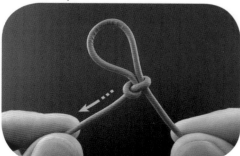

3. …and tighten, leaving a loop in the Slip Knot made.

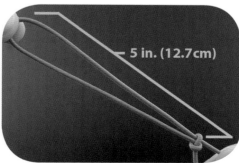

4. Pull the loop of the Slip Knot out 5 in. (12.7 cm).

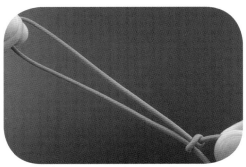

5. Flip the piece over, horizontally.

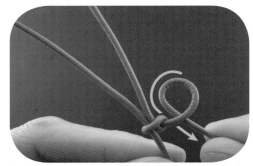

6. Make a clockwise loop with the cord on the right.

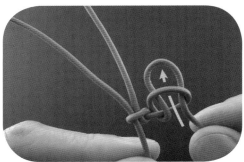

7. Bight the right running end through the loop…

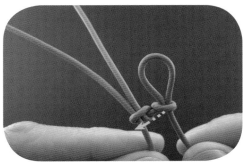

8. …and tighten, leaving a 0.5 in. (1.3 cm) loop in the Slip Knot made.

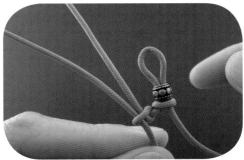

9. Place a bead with a 4 mm hole (minimum hole size) around the base of the loop.

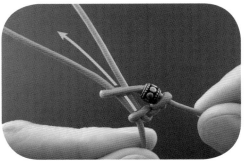

10. Insert the left loop through the front of the loop on the right.

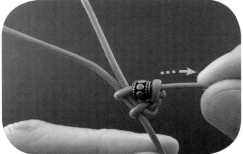

11. Tighten the beaded Slip Knot, leaving a slight bit of slack in its loop (i.e., portion around the left loop).

12. Repeat Steps 6 through 11 twelve more times.

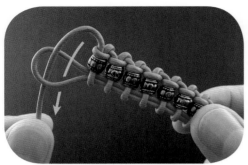

13. Insert the cord on the right through the front of the left loop.

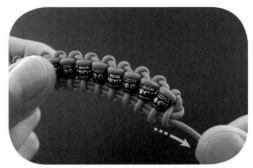

14. Pull on the cord at the opposite end of the piece until the left loop cinches closed.

15. Hook both ends of the piece into a downward facing **U**.

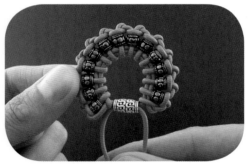

16. Ladder Stitch (see Page 17) a bead (see Step 9) around the left and right cord ends.

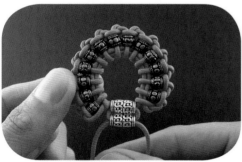

17. Repeat Step 16.

18. Flip the piece over, upside down…

19. …and shape it, until the void at its center is circular.

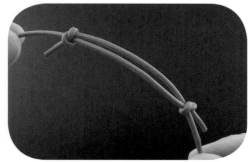

20. Tie a Fisherman's Knot (see Pages 23 and 24) with the cord ends to generate an adjustable necklace.

Beaded Aztec Sun Bar

Cords Used: One 7 ft. (2.1 m) & One 4 ft. (1.2 m), 2 mm Dia. Cord

Piece Size: 7.5 in. (19.1 cm) Bracelet

Beads Used: Thirteen 8x7 mm Cylindrical Beads, 5 mm Dia. Hole (Heart & Diamond Pattern)

Component Parts: Endless Falls + Lark's Head Knot + Bead Flourishes

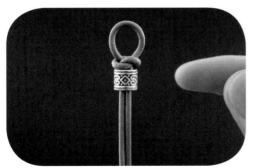

1. At the middle of the long cord, tie the Beaded Wall Knot Start (see Pages 1 and 2).

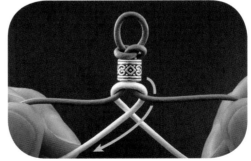

2. At the middle of the short cord, cross the right cord end over the left, behind and between the legs of the other cord.

3. Circle the upper cords around the back of the crossed cords, between the legs above.

4. Adjust the cords until the piece is firm.

5. Hook the middlemost right cord right, under the outer right cord.

6. Then circle it around the front of the outer right cord, exiting below itself.

7. Hook the middlemost left cord left, under the outer left cord.

8. Then circle it around the front of the outer left cord, exiting below itself.

9. Place a bead with a 4 mm hole (minimum hole size) around the middlemost cords.

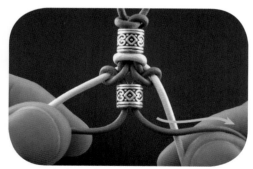

10. Hook the middlemost right cord right, over the outer right cord.

11. Then circle it around the back of the outer right cord, exiting above itself.

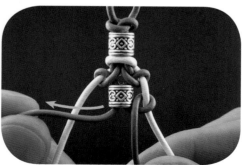

12. Hook the middlemost left cord left, over the outer left cord.

13. Then circle it around the back of the outer left cord, exiting above itself.

14. Repeat Steps 2 through 4, disregarding the initial positioning of the short cord in Step 2.

15. Repeat Steps 5 through 14 until a minimum 10 in. (25.4 cm) of cord ends remain.

16. Place a bead with a 5 mm hole (minimum hole size) around all four cords.

17. Make sure the middlemost cords in Step 15 are on top of the outer cords in Step 15.

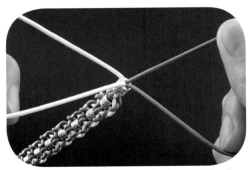

18. Flip the piece over, upside down and splay the cord ends out as shown.

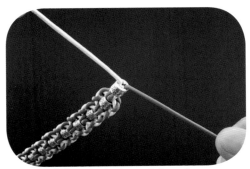

19. Carefully snip the lower left and upper right cord ends at the bead.

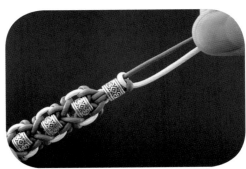

20. Firmly tie a 2-Strand Wall Knot (see Page 1) snugly atop the bead, with the remaining cords.

21. Tie a Double Overhand Knot (see Pages 2 and 3) 0.25 in. (0.64 cm) above the Wall Knot.

22. Carefully snip both cord ends 0.25 in. (0.64 cm) above the Double Overhand Knot.

DECODED
Ladder Stitching

Ladder stitching (see Page 17) allows a series of beads to be set parallel to one another (see Page 38). Primarily used in this book as a means by which to stabilize the finish of a knot or tie, the stitching technique can also, in itself, be used to create an attractive bead focused piece, as shown below.

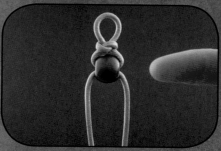

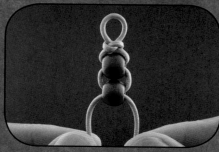

1. At the middle of the cord tie a Beaded Wall Knot Start (see Pages 1 and 2), Ladder Stitching (see Page 17) the bead.

2. Continue Ladder Stitching beads (see Page 17), one after another…

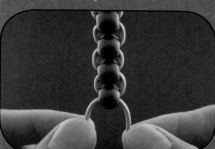

3. …until a minimum 10 in. (25.4 cm) of cord ends remain.

4. Tie a Double Overhand Knot (see Pages 2 and 3) 0.25 in. (0.64 cm) below the last placed bead.

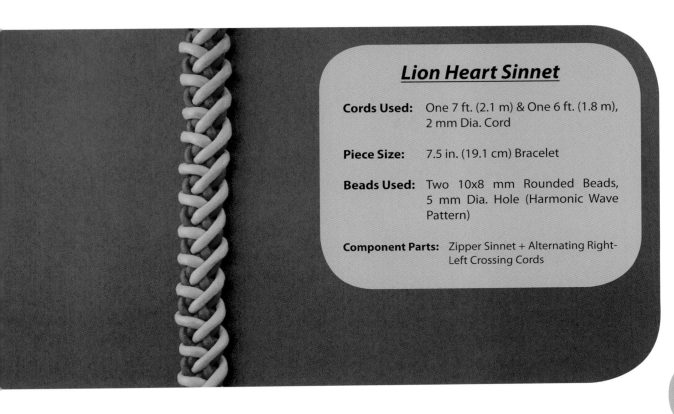

Lion Heart Sinnet

Cords Used: One 7 ft. (2.1 m) & One 6 ft. (1.8 m), 2 mm Dia. Cord

Piece Size: 7.5 in. (19.1 cm) Bracelet

Beads Used: Two 10x8 mm Rounded Beads, 5 mm Dia. Hole (Harmonic Wave Pattern)

Component Parts: Zipper Sinnet + Alternating Right-Left Crossing Cords

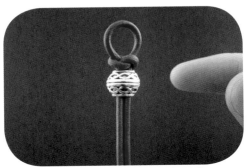

1. At the middle of the first cord, tie the Beaded Wall Knot Start (see Pages 1 and 2).

2. Flip the piece over, upside down.

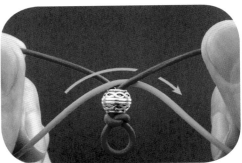

3. Lace the middle of the short cord over the left leg and under the right leg of the other cord.

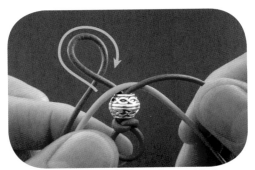

4. Make a counterclockwise loop with the outer left cord.

5. Bight the outer right cord through the left loop…

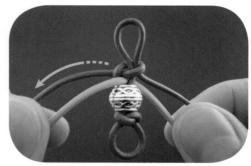

6. …and tighten, leaving a 0.5 in. (1.3 cm) loop in the Slip Knot made.

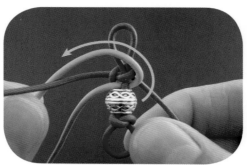

7. Hook the middlemost right cord left, over the front of the piece, between the outer left cord and the right loop.

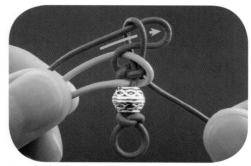

8. Bight the outer left cord, over the cord above, through the right loop…

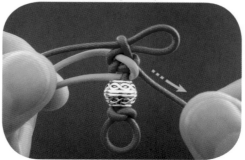

9. …and tighten, leaving a 0.5 in. (1.3 cm) loop in the Slip Knot made.

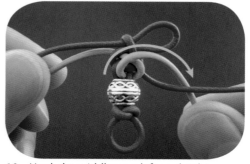

10. Hook the middlemost left cord right, over the front of the piece, between the outer right cord and the left loop.

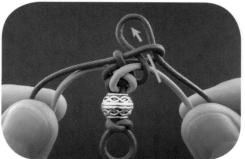

11. Bight the outer right cord, over the cord above, through the left loop…

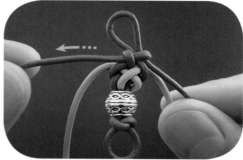

12. …and tighten, leaving a 0.5 in. (1.3 cm) loop in the Slip Knot made.

44

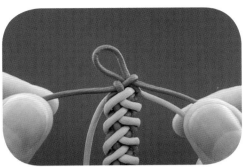

13. Repeat Steps 7 through 12 until a minimum 10 in. (25.4 cm) of cord ends remain.

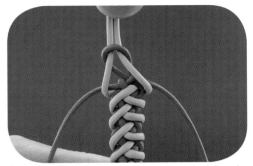

14. Then insert the middlemost cords through the loop above…

15. …and tighten firmly.

16. Place a bead with a 5 mm hole (minimum hole size) around all four cords.

17. Make sure the middlemost cords in Step 15 are on top of the outer cords in Step 15.

18. Flip the piece over, upside down and splay the cord ends out as shown.

19. Carefully snip the lower left and upper right cord ends at the bead.

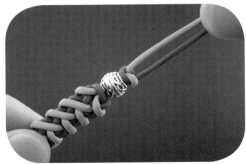

20. Firmly tie a 2-Strand Wall Knot (see Page 1) snugly atop the bead, with the remaining cords.

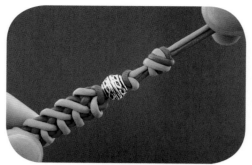

21. Tie a Double Overhand Knot (see Pages 2 and 3) 0.25 in. (0.64 cm) above the Wall Knot.

22. Carefully snip both cord ends 0.25 in. (0.64 cm) above the Double Overhand Knot.

DECODED
Zipper Sinnet

A sinnet is a weaving technique or tie generally (but not always) performed with a series of slip knots, that is used to shorten the length of a line. The two sinnets shown in this book, the Chained Arrow Sinnet and the Lion Heart Sinnet, are decorative sinnets built upon a more functional, yet still attractive, historical tying technique known as a Zipper Sinnet. To make a Zipper Sinnet on its own, follow the instructions below.

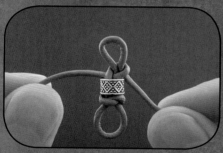

1. Follow Steps 1 through 6 on Pages 43 and 44, with the exception of Step 3, and disregard all future references to "middlemost" cords.

2. Repeat Steps 8 through 12 on Page 44 until a minimum 10 in. (25.4 cm) of cord ends remain.

3. Insert the left cord through the loop above and tighten firmly.

4. Tie a Double Overhand Knot (see Pages 2 and 3) 0.25 in. (0.64 cm) above cinched left cord.

Plum Blossom Dream Catcher

Cords Used: One 6 ft. (1.8 m) & One 4 ft. (1.2 m), 2 mm Dia. Cord

Piece Size: 4 in. (10.2 cm) Pendant Top to End of Tassels; 2.5 ft. (0.8 m) Adjustable Length Necklace

Beads Used: One 12x10 mm Rounded Bead, 5 mm Dia. Hole (Plated Resin); One 8x5 mm Cylindrical Beads, 5 mm Dia. Hole (Geometric Pattern); Two 7x9 mm Cylindrical Beads, 4 mm Dia. Hole (Reflected S Pattern)

Component Parts: Chinese Plum Blossom Knot + Snake Knot Tassels + Bead Flourishes

47

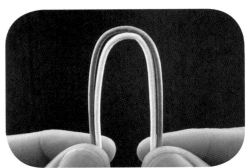

1. At the middle of both cords, doubled (short cord on top of long), make a bight.

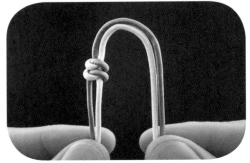

2. With the left cord ends, tie two 2-Strand Wall Knots (see Page 1), 0.5 in. (1.3 cm) below the top of the bight.

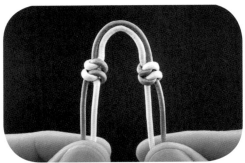

3. Repeat Step 2 with the right cord ends.

4. Place a bead with a 4 mm hole (minimum hole size) around each set of cord ends, below their respective Wall Knots.

5. Tie a 2-Strand Wall Knot - Around Cords (see Page 22), 1.0 in. (2.5 cm) below the beads.

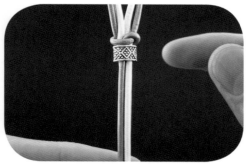

6. Place a bead with a 5 mm hole (minimum hole size) around all four cords…

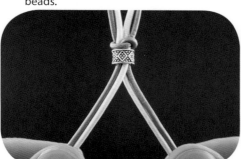

7. …making sure the outer and inner cords in Step 5 remain in position.

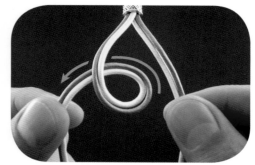

8. Make a clockwise **P** with the left doubled cord ends.

9. Drop the right doubled cord ends down over the loop of the **P**.

10. Hook the right (doubled) running ends left, over the leg of the **P**.

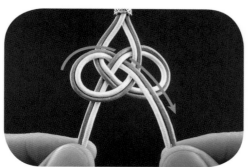

11. Then weave the running ends over, under, and over the doubled cords to the right.

12. Cross the doubled cord ends, right over left.

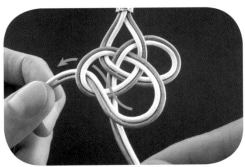

13. Insert the left running ends through the front of the left crook above. Then hook them to the right…

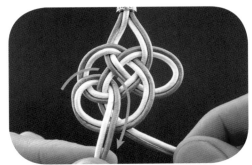

14. …under the doubled cords to the right and over the doubled cords below, exiting in front of the piece.

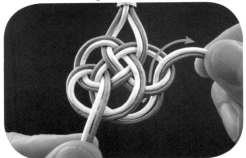

15. Insert the right running ends through the back of the right crook above. Then hook them to the left…

16. …over the doubled cords to the left and under the doubled cords below, exiting in front of the piece.

17. Cross the right doubled cords over the left.

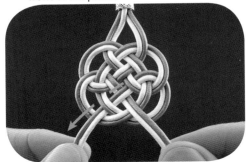

18. Then weave them under and over the doubled cords below.

19. Then weave the other set of doubled cords over and under the cords below them.

20. Adjust the cord ends until the Plum Blossom Knot is firm.

49

Leather Corded Fusion Ties

21. Tie a 2-Strand Wall Knot - Around Cords (see Page 22).

22. Drop the running ends of the Wall Knot down, between the middlemost cords.

23. Place a bead (see Step 6) around all four cords.

24. Flip the piece over, upside down and splay the cord ends out as shown.

25. Carefully snip the lower left and upper right cord ends at the bead.

26. Firmly tie a 2-Strand Wall Knot (see Page 1) snugly atop the bead, with the remaining cords.

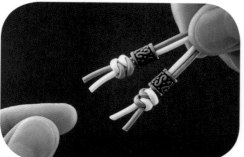

27. At the other end of the piece, carefully snip the bight in half. Make sure to leave a minimum 0.5 in. (1.3 cm) of cord ends.

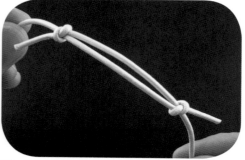

28. Tie a Fisherman's Knot (see Pages 23 and 24) with the cord ends to generate an adjustable necklace.

50

Noble Heart Knot

Cords Used: One 4 ft. (1.2 m), 2 mm Dia. Cord

Piece Size: 1.25 in. (3.8 cm) Dia. Pendant; 2.5 ft. (0.8 m) Adjustable Length Necklace

Beads Used: One 8x9 mm Cylindrical Bead, 5 mm Dia. Hole (Compressed Wave Pattern)

Component Parts: Big Celtic Heart Knot + Keyhole Technique + Bead Flourish

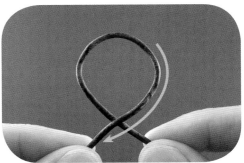

1. At the middle of the cord, make a clockwise loop.

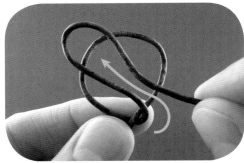

2. Bight the right cord end diagonally left, over the top of the loop.

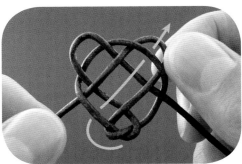

3. Bight the left cord end diagonally right, weaving it under, over-over, and under the cords above it.

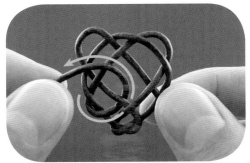

4. Hook the left running end up, diagonally right, weaving it over and under the cords above it.

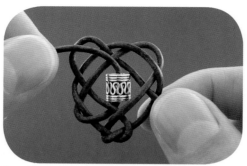

5. Place a bead with a 4 mm hole (minimum hole size) around the left running end, above the second diagonal cord.

6. Then hook the left running end diagonally left, weaving it over, under, and over the cords above it.

7. Hook the right running end up, diagonally left, weaving it under and over the cords above it.

8. Insert the right running end through the bead above it.

9. Then hook the right running end diagonally right, weaving it under, over, and under the cords above it.

10. Adjust the cord ends until the Noble Heart Knot is firm.

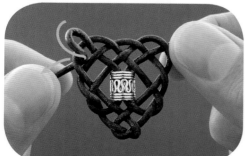

11. Knot Stabilization Tech.: Hook the left running end back, over and around the cord below it, leaving a small bight.

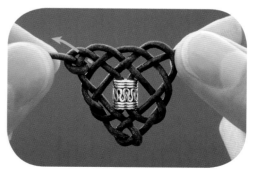

12. Then insert the running end through the back of the bight.

52

13. Hook the right running end back, under and around the cord below it, leaving a small bight.

14. Then insert the running end through the front of the bight.

15. Adjust the cord ends until the (Stabilized) Noble Heart Knot is firm.

16. Tie a Fisherman's Knot (see Pages 23 and 24) with the cord ends to generate an adjustable necklace.

DECODED
Mixing & Matching Techniques

Fusion knotting is the creation of innovative knots and ties through the merging of different knot elements or knotting techniques. Aside from being a means by which to create new knots and ties, the principles of fusion knotting allow a tyer to generate variant ties (i.e., similar, but different, completed pieces), by mixing tying techniques together. This can be done with nearly all the ties presented in this book. However, for guidance and inspiration, the following examples are provided.

1. Round Ribcage Braid: 4-Strand Round Braid (see Page 8) and Ribcage Braid (see Page 18) tying techniques.

2. Meandering Snake Braid: Meandering Lark's Head Braid (see Page 25) and Snake Weave (see Page 12) tying techniques.

Author Info

About the Author

© Ash Gerry

J.D. Lenzen is the creator of the highly acclaimed YouTube channel *Tying It All Together* and the producer of over 400 instructional videos. He's been formally recognized by the International Guild of Knot Tyers (IGKT) for his contributions to knotting, and is the originator of fusion knotting—the creation of innovative knots and ties through the merging of different knot elements or knotting techniques. *Leather Corded Fusion Ties* is Lenzen's sixth knot instruction book. *Decorative Fusion Knots*, *Paracord Fusion Ties - Volume 1*, *Paracord Fusion Ties - Volume 2*, *Paracord Project Inspirations*, and *Paracord Critters* are also available. He lives and works in San Francisco, California.

Acknowledgements

For their support and/or inspiration in the production of this book, the author would like to thank Clifford W. Ashley, Young Mike Stern, Steve Davis, Dale Gillespie, Ashley Somers, Bob and Sharon Kakos, Jon Olav Fivelstad, the country of Iceland and the members of the fusion knotting community as a whole. Without you, especially those who continue to support my books and online videos, this book would not have come to be.

And…

A special thanks to Ash Gerry for her design inspiration and unwavering support through each stage of book production.

A very special thanks to my wife and layout production artist, Kristen Kakos. Your presence in my life brings me joy, comfort and the freedom to create. For these gifts I am forever grateful.

Other 4th Level Indie Books

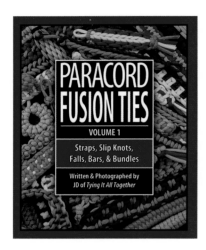

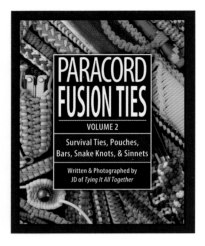

Paracord Fusion Ties - Volume 1
Straps, Slip Knots, Falls, Bars, & Bundles

ISBN: 978-0-9855578-0-5
8" x 10" Softcover

Published 2012

Paracord Fusion Ties - Volume 2
Survival Ties, Pouches, Bars, Snake Knots, & Sinnets

ISBN: 978-0-9855578-3-6
8" x 10" Softcover

Published 2013

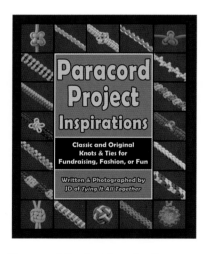

Paracord Project Inspirations
Classic and Original Knots & Ties for Fundraising, Fashion, or Fun

ISBN: 978-0-9855578-6-7
8" x 10" Softcover

Published 2014

Paracord Critters
Animal Shaped Knots & Ties

ISBN: 978-0-9855578-9-8
8" x 8" Softcover

Published 2015